THE HISTORY OF CHINA
IN 50 EVENTS

BY
Henry Freeman

Table of Contents

868 CE - Printing is Invented

960 CE - Sung Dynasty

1040 CE - Magnetic Compass Invented

1271 CE - Marco Polo Travels to China

1271 CE - Yuan Dynasty

1279 CE - Mongols Rule China

1368 CE - Ming Dynasty

1420 CE - The Forbidden City is Completed

1421 CE - Chinese Explorers Reach North America

1602 CE - The Dutch East India Company Starts
Trading in China

1644 CE - Qing Dynasty

1757 CE - The Canton System Adopted

Modern History

1839 CE - First Opium War

1900 CE - Boxer Rebellion

1911 CE - The Republic of China Holds First
Elections

1934 CE - The Long March

1937 CE - Nanking Massacre

1949 CE - The Republic of China Moves to Taiwan

1958 CE - The Great Leap Forward

1966 CE - The Cultural Revolution

1972 CE - Nixon Visits China

1989 CE - Tiananmen Square Protests

2002 CE - SARS Outbreak

2003 CE - First Manned Chinese Spaceflight

2008 CE - Beijing Olympics Held

Ancient History

"The strength of a nation derives from the integrity of the home."

—Confucius

125,000 BCE - Homo Sapiens First Appear in China

In c.130,000 BCE, the northern hemisphere entered the Eemian interglacial period of the most current Ice Age. During this period, the average temperature was as much as two degrees warmer than the modern period. As such, it encouraged the migration of various species, in particular Homo sapiens. More than other Homo species, Homo sapiens demonstrated adaptability and ingenuity. The Eemian period made habitable portions of the world that would have previously not supported human life, and Homo sapiens took advantage of the climate shift. Approximately five thousand years later, a group of hunter-gatherer humans made the journey across central Asia and reached what is today recognized as China. Over the next several tens of thousands of years, these early hunter-gatherers began to establish permanent settlements. With this settlement, the basis for the tribes that became the Chinese was established.

7600 BCE - Pigs First Domesticated

One of the most important milestones that a culture can reach during its early history is the domestication of animals. This process allows a society to move from hunter-gatherer to agrarian, which provides stability for the people. After a civilization has moved to an agrarian lifestyle, they have the opportunity to focus on language development, which is the first step in establishing permanence of culture.

In China, the earliest record of domestication points to roughly 7600 BCE as the time when the Chinese first domesticated pigs. The value of domesticating pigs over other animals is manifold. First, pigs possess a high level of intelligence, meaning that farmers need not spend time supervising the animals, making the farmer more productive. Second, pigs are omnivorous, which reduces the land required to graze a herd of animals. As such, pigs can be raised in relatively small areas, increasing the yield for a given space. When the Chinese first domesticated pigs, it was their general tractability that made the pig a desirable candidate for domestication. As the process of domestication was mastered, it allowed the Chinese to domesticate other animals, so that the diversity of "farmable" animals increased drastically. As is almost always the case when the food supply surpasses the needs of the civilization, citizens were able to move beyond farming to perfect the myriad skills required in a technological society.

3000 BCE - The Plow is First Used in China

In order to produce the abundant food supply required for a society to move from agrarian to technological pursuits, advancements in farming techniques are key. To increase the amount of a crop that can be grown, it is necessary to prepare the soil to maximize aeration and nutrient dispersion. Before 3000 BCE, this tilling of the land was done by hand, with a form of pick or hoe. The Chinese, however, discovered that a fixed blade could be attached to a frame, and pulled through the earth, allowing a much greater area of land to be cultivated for significantly less effort and time.

Initially, plows were pulled by farmers, but, thanks to the domestication of animals, plows could be harnessed to beasts of burden, greatly reducing the effort needed to farm an area of land and effectively increasing the area of land that a farmer could oversee. This increase, in turn, led to the production of ever greater volumes of food, allowing for the diversification of occupation required in an advanced society. The emergence of the plow signaled the beginning of a modern Chinese society, and it was the first of many inventions that would revolutionize the farming industry to benefit the Chinese society as a whole.

2500 BCE - The Battle of Banquan

The Battle of Banquan holds a place in Chinese history as it is the first recorded battle in China. Although much of the historical record is clouded on the subject, it is believed that the battle was fought in 2500 BCE. History, or legend, indicates that the battle was fought between the forces of Huangdi, known as the Yellow Emperor, and the forces of Yandi, known as the Flame Emperor. The battle likely took place in the province of Shanxi, but tradition holds that the battle was fought near the city of Banquan, located near modern-day Beijing. Nevertheless, the Flame Emperor was defeated and made peace with the Yellow Emperor.

The two tribes merged over time, and this merger is credited as the beginning of Han China. Han is the largest ethnic group among the Chinese, accounting for more than 90 percent of the total population of China. This battle is therefore not only famous for being first but also for unifying the major Chinese tribes, further demonstrating that peace among the tribes was preferable to warfare. This view was an indicator that the Chinese felt secure in their borders; they had developed enough to protect themselves without having to use force.

2200 BCE - The Great Flood Occurs

In approximately 2200 BCE, both the Yellow and Yangtze River valleys flooded. The scope of the flood was such that the day-to-day operation of the Chinese government was stalled in an effort to contain the flooding. It is believed that the flood lasted for two generations until Emperor Yu enacted a policy of drainage instead of simply trying to contain the waters. As with much of early Chinese history, a great deal of the historical records are intertwined with myth, making the task of separating the two difficult. Historians view the account of the Great Flood as an insight into the culture of early Chinese society, as, with other early civilizations, the myths told were reflective of a culture's beliefs and ways of thinking. As such, historians gather a great understanding of the importance of family and hero mythology from these stories, and it is these same themes that remain important throughout much of Chinese literature and history. In any event, Emperor Yu, according to the story, founded the Xia Dynasty once the flood waters had receded.

2100 BCE - Xia Dynasty

The Great Flood of 2200 BCE was such a cataclysmic event that, upon its recession, Yu was able to forge the first dynasty in Chinese history. The Xia Dynasty held sway in China from 2100 to 1600 BCE. During the Xia Dynasty, the Xia began a practice that would affect dynastic China throughout much of history. This practice is the belief in an idea known as the Mandate of Heaven. The Mandate (which had no official name until several dynasties later) was the idea that a dynasty derived its right to rule from heaven, thus making it impossible for more than one dynasty to exist at a given time. The Mandate became the basis for all subsequent dynasties and helps explain why future dynasties went to such great lengths to suppress information about previous dynasties. If a dynasty was merely a follow-on, then clearly it was not mandated from a deity, thus opening up the possibility of it being supplanted by a successor.

Due to the practice of the Mandate, reliable written sources from the Xia do not exist, leaving only archaeological evidence to provide a glimpse into the dynasty. Modern archaeology suggests that the Xia Dynasty might have existed alongside a second empire, but that due to similarities between the two, it would be almost impossible to tell them apart. If true, these dual empires would cast suspicion on the Mandate of Heaven, and it is possible that the Xia, in an effort to suppress this knowledge, redacted their own written works to prevent dynastic succession. Despite this, the archaeological record does indicate that at least one empire existed at the time and location that history ascribes to the Xia, meaning that the Xia can rightfully claim its place as the first Chinese empire.

1600 BCE - Shang Dynasty

It is often the case with dynastic rule that, as centuries pass, the rulers of the dynasty succumb to weakness of character. This is often followed by an unwillingness to defend and provide for the dynasty, thus paving the way for dynastic succession. Such was the case with the Xia Dynasty. Its final ruler was defeated in the Battle of Mingtiao, at which time, the Shang Dynasty was founded. The dynasty held sway in the Yellow River Valley for the course of its five-hundred-year reign.

The Shang Dynasty is remembered for many things, but perhaps most important is that the earliest Chinese writing comes from the Shang. The Shang wrote important information on oracle bones, as much of their culture was dependent on divination. The Shang also became the first dynasty to work extensively in bronze, and thanks to the tombs of the emperors, much of this bronze has been unearthed, giving a very accurate portrayal of the myriad uses of bronze in the dynasty. The Shang also began using chariots, and this suggests that at some point the Shang had contact with societies to the west, particularly the Middle East, but sadly, no record of this contact exists. Eventually, a rival to the Shang emerged and defeated the Shang in battle. Legend holds that the last Shang king killed himself after the defeat, leaving an open throne that would be claimed by the Zhou.

1046 BCE - Zhou Dynasty

After the defeat of the Shang, the Zhou Dynasty was begun. The Zhou Dynasty was the longest-lived in Chinese history, spanning eight hundred years. During the Zhou period, the importance of bronze was increased, causing this era to be considered the height of the Bronze Age in China. The Zhou were the first to give a name to the Mandate of Heaven, and in order to legitimize their own position, retroactively applied the term to the Xia and Shang.

Under the Zhou, China entered a period of feudalism, which is a system of power and wealth based on land ownership. This period is analogous to the Middle Ages in Europe when a similar system was in use. It was during the Zhou Dynasty that some of China's most influential thinkers lived, including Confucius, Lao tzu, and Sun tzu. The Zhou also standardized written language into a shape similar to its modern form. In addition, the Zhou began using reservoirs as a source of crop irrigation, meaning that farming could be moved inland from flowing water sources, helping to alleviate the problem of flooding. Historians consider the Zhou Dynasty to be the peak of classical Chinese civilization, thanks to contributions in so many fields.

551 BCE - Confucius is Born

One of the most influential Chinese thinkers, Confucius, was born at the height of the Zhou Dynasty. Confucius is perhaps most well known for his work in social relationships and social contract. A system of thinking, Confucianism is named after him and espouses his Five Relationships, which, if followed, were intended to bring peace and prosperity throughout China. These relationships were: father-to-son, brother-to-brother, husband-to-wife, peer-to-peer, and king-to-subject. For each of these relationships, Confucius ascribed a set of attitudes and actions to follow. The purpose of these attitudes and actions was to eliminate emotional thinking, which, to Confucius was at the heart of societal struggle.

Although many have followed Confucius as a religious leader, his work speaks more like a socio-political treatise than religion. In fact, despite supporting traditions such as ancestor worship, Confucius focused his efforts and writing on secular matters. The followers of Confucius spread his works, and after his death in 479 BCE, his philosophy began to be adapted into a set of religious practices and principles. His work became one of the pivotal ideologies of the Hundred Schools of Thought of the Zhou Dynasty. Confucius' work is still studied today, and elements of his work can be found in modern governmental and business practices.

c.551 BCE - Lao Tzu is Born

Another of China's most important philosophers was a contemporary of Confucius. Lao Tzu, or Laozi, tended toward a more spiritual understanding of the world, and as such, his work reflects these ideas. As another key pillar in the Hundred Schools of Thought, the work of Lao Tzu is considered of similar or equal value to Confucius.

Lao Tzu is most well known for being the founder of Taoism. Taoism is centered upon two major ideas: Wu wei and yin-yang. Wu wei is a concept of non-action, where a person will find peace through quiet inaction, rather than a search to change circumstances. Yin-yang, which has become a pop culture symbol in many western countries is a philosophy of equal opposites. Although often represented as a light/dark dichotomy, the philosophy actually embraces the idea that for any given thing, its opposite is central to its makeup. For example, a tree is strong, but cannot withstand a hurricane; a blade of grass is weak, but remains when the storm has passed. As a philosophy, the yin-yang is an attempt to acknowledge the fluidity found in nature and the harm that can be caused by stasis. Lao Tzu believed that in embracing these two ideas, people would find peace and harmony with nature.

548 BCE - "Go" Game is First Played

Games have always been an important method of understanding a culture, and its values and structures. The game of "Go" is no exception. First played in 548 BCE, the game influenced, and was influenced by, thinkers such as Confucius and Lao Tzu. At its most basic, the game is a strategy game similar to chess in that it stresses positional supremacy. Unlike chess which has a set of permissible moves, the game of Go has very few rules. In the game, adaptability and patience are the most valued traits, and as such, the contest is often much less about the game itself than about the contest of wills between players. Go was seen as such an important analogy for life that during the time of Confucius, mastery of the game was considered to be a prerequisite for the literati and political leaders. The game has been passed down through history, and although not of great popularity in the western hemisphere, continues to be one of the most-often played games in eastern Asia. The game continues to be a mirror of dominant eastern philosophies, and as such, provides an excellent glimpse into the cultures that traditionally play the game.

544 BCE - Sun Tzu is Born

Another contemporary of Confucius was the military leader and strategist Sun Tzu. Most famous for his work the *Art of War*, Sun Tzu is credited for creating empathetic warfare, whereby understanding an enemy would inevitably lead to their defeat. The book is a treatise on the formation, equipping, training, and leading of an army. Sun Tzu's work delves into many non-military aspects of life, as he believed that knowledge was the most effective weapon and that a leader with more knowledge could defeat another leader with a larger army.

Sun Tzu's work has become a common philosophical cornerstone for such diverse things as business management, sports strategy, and political science. The book was designed to dovetail with Lao Tzu's work, and Sun Tzu saw the practices in his work as merely a physical extension of the Taoist philosophy. As such, Sun Tzu believed that someone unpracticed in Taoism would miss the subtlety of his work, leading to a misunderstanding of the work. This meant that Sun Tzu could publish the work freely, as someone without a Taoist background would not be able to exploit the work in battle against Sun Tzu and the Chinese army. In many respects, Sun Tzu is considered to be the father of modern military strategy.

500 BCE - Cast Iron Invented

Steel is a prized material for its strength, hardness, and light weight. However, steel making is a very complex process, and, particularly prior to the Industrial Revolution, was very expensive, both in terms of materials and labor. As the Chinese sought a cheaper alternative, they stumbled upon the substance known as cast iron. Although cast iron is heavier and weaker than steel, it is significantly easier to produce. The primary advantage of cast iron over steel is that it can be molded at significantly lower temperatures.

The name cast iron comes from the fact that the substance is very brittle, and does not handle traditional ironworking without cracking. To that end, cast iron, as the name suggests, must be cast into a predetermined shape, and, once in that shape, cannot be formed into another without re-melting the iron. However, for non-military applications, cast iron is an excellent substitute for steel, particularly in domestic situations. By producing large quantities of cast iron for civilian use, the Chinese freed up their steel production for military and infrastructure purposes. Although not a revolutionary technology, the application of cast iron was certainly revolutionary and spurred a quest for similar substitute materials that could be provided cheaply to civilians.

259 BCE - Shihuangdi is Born

In 259 BCE, the son of Prince Yiren of Qin was born. In 246 BCE, Yiren died, leaving the throne of Qin to his son, known as Shihuangdi or Zhao Zeng. However, being 13 years old, Zeng was not prepared to rule, and a regent was appointed for him. His regent was Lu Buwei, the man responsible for helping his father ascend the throne. When Buwei was implicated in an assassination attempt on Zeng's life, he drank a cup of poison to escape legal proceedings. At that point, Zeng assumed full control of his state.

Zeng set out on a conquest almost immediately, and by 230 BCE, Zeng's army began capturing neighboring states. His army conquered Han, Zhao, Yan, Wei, and Chu. When Zeng finally captured the state of Qi, he took the title emperor instead of king as his predecessors had done. He did this to celebrate the unification of China into an empire. Zeng, who took the name Shihuangdi, set out on a program of social, economic, and political reform. He abolished the feudal system and instead reorganized his empire into military districts. Under this system, a meritocracy was established, promoting talent whenever it was found. Shihuangdi standardized the written language of China, as well as its system of weights and measures. Doing so promoted economic growth and prosperity. He also started building a national road system and began unifying a series of smaller walls into the Great Wall. He is also responsible for commissioning the famous Terra Cotta Army to guard his massive tomb.

221 BCE - Ch'in Dynasty

Emperor Shihuangdi unified China in 221 BCE, and this marked the beginning of the Ch'in Empire. The modern name "China" is derived from Ch'in, which demonstrates the importance placed on this seminal event. The Ch'in, seeking to discredit previous empires and kingdoms within China, began the practice of destroying the historical record of previous dynasties. This practice, which was continued by later empires, has made the study of China more difficult, as a great deal of the written record was destroyed. The Ch'in also attempted to suppress Confucianism, as it was seen as being too independent, and the Ch'in sought to create a highly dependent citizenry. Much of the effort of the Ch'in was expended on infrastructure, notably the Great Wall, and a national highway system. These efforts, along with military action outside of the Chinese border, meant that arts and education were given short shrift. Despite its military prowess, the Ch'in Dynasty only last for 15 years.

220 BCE - The Great Wall is Begun

As early as 700 BCE, kingdoms within China had begun the practice of buildings vast walls as a means of protection from invasion. When Shihuangdi united China, he began a project to unify and expand the walls that already existed. During this time, the Chinese built on the wall extensively. Even though no written record exists that gives exact dimensions for the Ch'in wall, it is estimated that somewhere between 100,000 and 1,000,000 people died during its construction. The expanded wall played an important role in defense, but also in trade—the wall made toll collection possible, and artificially created trade routes that were favorable to the Ch'in.

The parts of the wall that exists today were mostly created during the Ming Dynasty. When considering all of the branches of the wall that have been created, the approximate length of the wall is 13,000 miles long. The wall in most places is between 15 and 20 feet high, with a width of at least 15 feet across the top. This width was designed to allow defenders to move quickly and easily between fortifications in the event of an invasion. Despite the fact that much of the wall has been destroyed or fallen into decay, it remains as a man-made structure that is visible from space. The Great Wall was a demonstration of Chinese prowess in engineering throughout much of China's history.

210 BCE - The Terra Cotta Army is Created

In 1974, farmers were digging a well and broke through into a chamber containing a series of lifelike terra cotta figures. Archaeologists began excavating the site and realized that this was the famed Terra Cotta Army that Shihuangdi had created to guard his mausoleum. Shihuangdi had assigned as many as 700,000 people to build the burial site, and, wanting to guard it, he commissioned an entire army of terra cotta soldiers.

Modern estimates reveal that the army had as many as 8,000 soldiers, several hundred horsemen, as well as other figures including entertainers.

This army served two purposes. Firstly, to protect the emperor's tomb from exploration or theft, and secondly, to provide the emperor with a retinue in the afterlife. It was assumed that the army would give Shihuangdi the preeminence in death that he had had in life. The mausoleum itself was the size of a small city, and so it seems that Shihuangdi wanted an army to match the greatness of his burial ground. Since its discovery, the tomb has not been opened, as there are fears that exposure to the air might ruin artifacts inside, and attempting to fully regulate the environment of a structure the size of a football field has as yet proven to be highly impractical. Whether the tomb is ever opened, the Terra Cotta Army has provided key insights into the life and reign of Shihuangdi.

206 BCE - Han Dynasty

After the end of the Ch'in Dynasty, the Han Dynasty took its place. The Han, an ethnic group of Chinese to which most modern Chinese citizens trace their descent, was the second imperial dynasty in Chinese history. Under the Han, who ruled until 220 CE, China entered a Golden Age—a time of prosperity, growth, and enlightenment. Under the Han, the emperor ruled with the help of advisors, most of whom were of noble birth. A system of coins was also introduced that was in use for almost eight hundred years.

The dynasty embraced the idea of a class-based society, wherein skill and effort could be rewarded by upward mobility. Although nobility was still based on lineage, this system encouraged hard work and innovation—which in turn was responsible for the Golden Age. Women had similar legal rights as men, which is fairly remarkable, given the legal rights of women in most of the concurrent western (or middle-eastern) societies.

In order to streamline the production of industrial goods like steel, the Han took privatized industries and placed them under government control. Over the course of the dynasty, this policy changed, but it was certainly efficient when it was conceived. The Han Dynasty came to an end when the last Han emperor was murdered by one of his generals. Still, the succeeding dynasty followed much of the precedent and practices established by the Han.

The Age of Invention

"If you stand by the pond and want the fish in it, you are better off going home to make a fish net than to continue standing by the pond."

—Dong Zhongshu

3 CE - National School System Implemented

Emperor Ping of the Han Dynasty sought the creation of an educated ministerial class of citizens who would be suited to the administration of his empire. As such, Ping instituted a national school system known as the Guozijian. These schools taught Confucianism and literature to students in order to prepare them for civil service. Although this school was not the first of its kind in China, it was the preeminent school and was not closed until 1905. The idea of public education was not unknown, but the scope of the Chinese education was much broader than a comparable education elsewhere in the world at that time. This school system became a model for others, and even though merit-based positions in the government was uncommon for almost nine hundred years, the school did create a workforce of highly knowledgeable civil servants who continued to help the Han Dynasty (and others) flourish.

105 CE - Paper is Invented

The Golden Age of the Han Dynasty was a time of great scientific advancement. With a focus on education, the Han fostered a desire to explore and create. In 105 CE, the Han gave the world one of its most important contributions—papermaking. This date is somewhat suspect, as historical records indicate the very first mention of paper almost two hundred years earlier. But, whichever date is factually correct, it is not disputed that the Chinese discovered and perfected the art of papermaking.

The Chinese saw that wet tree bark, if flattened and dried, became an excellent medium for writing. After that, improvements to the process were made, including the use of different bark, softwood chips (pulp) as a paper source, and liquid emulsions to hold the paper together. Although papermaking remained a cottage industry for several hundred years, paper did not even reach Europe until 1150. In fact, the Chinese had invented printing before paper reached Europe for the first time. The value of paper to a society is that it is inexpensive, easy to manufacture, and the raw materials exist in overwhelming amounts. Prior to the invention of paper, most writing was done either on papyrus or vellum (dried animal skin). In either case, the labor to produce writing materials was extensive, and with vellum quite expensive, so that only the wealthy could afford to keep written records. With the advent of paper and printing, the availability of the printed word increased quickly, which in turn led to an increase in the overall education of a given population.

132 CE - Directional Seismometer Invented

Earthquakes have always presented problems to societies, but as a community becomes less rural, the potential for destruction increases. This is due to a shift in population and resource density that comes along with urban increase. In order to study earthquakes, a method of measuring and recording these events is necessary. In 132 CE, Zhang Heng invented a machine called a seismoscope (or seismometer). This device was a large drum that held a series of balls in the air at various points around the drum. If the earth moved, depending on the direction of motion and scale of motion, the drum would release a ball. The ball would be caught in a cup, and the resulting sound would indicate to a listener that an event had occurred. Although this device could not keep a record of events, it was able to help scientists learn about how the earth moved during an earthquake.

Despite the advancements in technology, all modern seismometers are based on this same principle—the suspension of a weight to indicate direction and intensity. The historical record shows that this first seismometer was able to measure an earthquake even though people in the same room could not feel the vibrations; it was a step toward further understanding how the earth functions, and how to keep people safe when interacting with nature.

142 CE - Gunpowder is Invented

The very earliest recorded reference to gunpowder came in 142 CE when a Chinese scholar wrote about various powders that when mixed together would "dance." By 492, the Chinese became aware that saltpeter (one of the main ingredients in gunpowder) could burn. In 1044, a formula for gunpowder was created, and it remains the earliest known record of gunpowder. With the invention of gunpowder, the Chinese found a substance with myriad uses. It could be used to make weapons (although not in a form that would be recognizable today), for construction or demolition, and entertainment (the Chinese also were the first to invent fireworks).

This substance was relatively easy to produce and stable to transport, meaning that it gained fairly wide-spread use in China. It was not until approximately 1200 that Europe first acquired knowledge of gunpowder, and it was not until significantly later that Europeans first put the substance to military use. Gunpowder is considered one of China's Four Great Inventions—inventions that were unique to the country and changed the world. Although many people in modern times believe that gunpowder is a new invention, it can be traced back to the Golden Age of the Han Dynasty.

166 CE - Romans First Reach China

As the Roman Empire expanded to the east, Romans first came in contact with traders on the Silk Road. Over time, as trade flourished, the Romans sought to establish trade relations with the source of the new goods, rather than rely on merchants to import them. In 166 CE, Marcus Aurelius sent a trade delegation along the Silk Road to make first contact. Later that year, Romans first reached China and established an embassy there. Although trade remained prosperous, linguistic and cultural difficulties prevented either side from making any real progress on inter-empire alliances. Further, the Chinese had such abundant resources that they had no real need of western goods, thus putting a damper on relations. Still, the Chinese were more than willing to sell goods to the Romans.

This first contact is important to history as it was the first time that China forayed into the world of international trade, and became a world superpower. Over time, Rome's reliance on China's luxury goods became so pervasive that the Roman Senate attempted to outlaw the use of specific luxury items. But the desire for these items was greater than the penalty for owning them, and the Senate tired of enforcing commercial regulations on its citizens. When this occurred, more goods than ever began to flow westward from China.

618 CE - Tang Dynasty

After the assassination of the last Han emperor, the emperor's cousin, Li Yuan, named himself the leader of the Tang Dynasty. The Dynasty lasted until 907 when a military governor overthrew the emperor. Much like the

Han, the Tang Dynasty was a time of much scientific learning. The Tang first invented printing, discovered diabetes and ways to lessen its symptoms, and created a system for generating highly sophisticated maps. The Tang gave women almost equal rights with men, although there is some question as to whether this applied to all women or simply those in urban areas. The Tang also had a passion for automated machinery that would perform very simple tasks. These inventions indicate a high level of sophistication and technical prowess, which, given the conditions in most of the rest of the world at the time, was highly advanced. The Tang also worked on a system to pipe cooking gas into the stoves inside the home. In terms of art, the Tang spent a great deal of time perfecting poetry to such an extent that one had to be highly proficient as a poet to gain employment as a civil servant. Overall, the Tang Dynasty was a time of peace and prosperity for China.

845 CE - Great Anti-Buddhist Persecution

In the wake of several unsuccessful battles, the Tang Dynasty ran short on money. At the same time, resentment towards Buddhists was growing, as Buddhism espoused several key principles that were antithetical to classical (Confucian) Chinese ideals. When coupled together, the facts gave the emperor an opportunity to deal with two problems simultaneously. In the early part of the persecution, the emperor demanded that Buddhist monks turn over their wealth to the state and that criminals and "sorcerers" not be allowed to remain monks.

After a year, the emperor, who was aging rapidly, decided to begin a program of extermination. To escape this program, monks were required to turn over their money and lands, before fleeing China. Upon the emperor's death, the persecution came to an end. Although the persecution only lasted two years, a great deal of damage had been done—not only to Buddhism but also to other organized religions in China. At that time, China began to move toward a much more secular culture. Although various religious groups would send missionaries to China, after the Great Persecution, religion in China never fully recovered to pre-Persecution levels.

868 CE - Printing is Invented

The last of the great Tang contributions was the invention of printing. In 868, a text known as the *Diamond Sutra* was printed onto a scroll that was 16 feet long. This scroll was formed by gluing the edges of several sheets of paper together. The book itself relates that it was printed on May 11, 868, allowing scholars to have an unprecedented understanding of the circumstances surrounding this book. The work is also important because it contains the first printed illustration. Although Johannes Gutenberg is credited with the first moveable-type printing press, early

Chinese printing predated Gutenberg by approximately 650 years.

The Chinese discovery of printing led to a boom in literacy as individuals could own inexpensive printed copies of seminal Chinese literature. At the same time, using paper as a printing medium meant that following empires would have an easy time getting rid of the written history of a dynasty. The basic method of printing—carving an image onto a medium and using that medium to transfer ink remains much unchanged into the modern world, and although innovations have been made, they have all simply been upgrades to the basic Chinese technique that was invented more than a thousand years ago.

960 CE - Sung Dynasty

Following the Tang Dynasty, the Sung Dynasty assumed power in 960. The dynasty lasted until 1279 when the Mongols completed their takeover of China and established the Yuan Dynasty. The Sung Dynasty, much like its predecessors, was a period of enlightenment and exploration. The Sung made many remarkable discoveries, not the least of which was a magnetic compass that was able to establish the cardinal direction of true north. In economic matters, the Sung Dynasty was the first government in history to issue a fully functional paper currency. This revolutionary practice not only changed the relationship of the nation to its wealth but provided the basis for an economic increase of vast proportions.

The Sung also created joint-stock corporations, in order to offset the cost and difficulty of financing international exploration. An expansive steel-making network enabled the Sung to create many different pieces of infrastructure, including the lock system of water transport. The Sung built canals to expedite trade within the empire. The Sung were the first to use gunpowder as a tool of war, which coupled to steel production, allowed the Sung to produce thousands of bombs (explosive projectiles). The Sung ruled for just over four hundred years, until a military force so vast that not even gunpowder could dispel it, conquered China.

1040 CE - Magnetic Compass Invented

One of the keys to successful exploration is the ability to keep track of one's current position, as well as the relative position of key landmarks. While maps are a useful tool in recording these findings, maps alone cannot keep an explorer in known lands. What is needed is a device for tracking changes in direction, so that an accurate record of a journey can be kept. The Han Dynasty first invented a form of compass sometime around 206 BCE but did not find a practical, long-distance use for it. The Sung Dynasty is credited with taking the magnet compass, which measures position in relation to a fixed object (the magnetic north pole). The Sung took their magnetic compass, and mounted it aboard ships, thus enabling sailors to track the direction in which they were sailing—crucial since the ocean by itself is quite empty and featureless, meaning that sailing in circles is a likely possibility. The magnetic compass allowed the Chinese to begin long-distance exploration, which would culminate in their discovery of North America in the early 1400s.

1271 CE - Marco Polo Travels to China

One of the most famous explorers in European history is Marco Polo. His work, *Book of the Marvels of the World*, was an inspiration for generations of explorers, including Christopher Columbus. While there is debate over the authenticity of the text of the book, for much of recent history, scholars have believed the book to be accurate. As such, the text is still used as source material, although often with a grain of salt.

In the book, Polo details the travels of himself and his family to China. According to him, Polo reached the summer residence of Kublai Khan, Mongol leader, and ruler of China (although the unification did not occur until 1279). Polo, in 1271, reached the palace and completed a diplomatic mission of his father. He then served as a government official until 1292, at which time he returned to Europe. Polo's book spoke in great detail about the marvels of Chinese society, and its many social, cultural, and scientific advances. His prose so lovingly described China that the book became an explorer's handbook of sorts. Whether or not the book is accurate, the impact Marco Polo had on future explorers cannot be ignored. He was a hero to many young Europeans and inspired whole nations to venture into the largely unknown realms of the Far East.

1271 CE - Yuan Dynasty

After several decades of ruling a large portion of northern China, in addition to Mongolia, Kublai Khan, the grandson of Genghis Khan, formally declared his rule in China a dynasty. Kublai Khan claimed that his grandfather had been the founder of the dynasty, and Khan sought to use the Mandate of Heaven to give his dynasty legitimacy in the eyes of his Chinese subjects. Khan's capital was located at Khanbaliq, modern-day Beijing.

One of the most important aspects of the Yuan Dynasty was its focus on international trade. As a small part of the Mongol Empire, the Yuan had access to the Silk Road, as well as vast portions of Asia and Europe. Due in large part to trade, the exposure to foreign cultures began to bring cultural diversity to China, which previously had been largely insular. The Yuan Dynasty, in seeking to enmesh itself with the captive culture chose to maintain a governmental system almost identical to the one in place in previous dynasties. The Yuan sought to maintain control over China without further military action, and as such, chose to adopt Chinese culture instead of requiring the Chinese to adapt to Mongol culture.

1279 CE - Mongols Rule China

Kublai Khan established the Yuan Dynasty in China in 1271. Over the next eight years, Khan spent vast resources bringing the small kingdoms around China into submission. These kingdoms, such as the Dali and Xi-Xia, were made up of ethnic Chinese who, for various reasons, had not been co-opted or coerced into the Chinese Empire. However, as the goal of the Mongol Empire was to control all of Asia, these smaller states needed to be conquered. In 1279, Khan finally brought them into the Chinese Empire, meaning that for the first time, all peoples of Chinese descent were united in a single empire.

The Yuan Dynasty was the first time that the Chinese Empire had been ruled by a foreigner, and although it would happen again with the Manchus, who founded the Qing Dynasty, the Yuan Dynasty represented the peak of foreign control of China. Perhaps more than at any other point in its history, the Yuan Dynasty was an exemplar of an empire in that a single ruler held sway over various peoples who maintained their cultural identity without merging into a new culture. When the Mongol Empire began struggling to maintain its borders, the Yuan leadership retreated to Mongolia, opening the way for the Ming Dynasty.

1368 CE - Ming Dynasty

As the Yuan Dynasty collapsed, a new dynasty, the Ming, took its place. The Ming ruled in China until 1644, when the Qing Dynasty gained ascendancy. Scholars consider the Ming Dynasty to be one of the premier examples of a peaceful and stable reign of any government in history. In order to protect the citizenry, the Ming began a massive project to repair and improve the Great Wall. Thanks to the efforts of the Ch'in, the dimensions of the Wall were well established. Instead of simply rebuilding the earthen walls that made up the wall, the Ming began fortifying it with brick and stone, turning it from a diversion into a massive fortification that would last until modern times. In fact, most of the Great Wall that is still standing was built by the Ming.

During the period of stability brought about by the Ming, many advances in artistic endeavors were made. Most notable was the ceramic work of the period. Chinese porcelain, which has become the world standard is so associated with its place of origin that in many western countries, it is simply referred to as "China." The Ming invented new techniques to fire porcelain, as well as methods for adorning it. For many people, the Ming are so associated with porcelain that the word instantly conjures images of a beautiful, if fragile, vase. Despite the stability and prosperity of the Ming, time eventually took its toll, and the Ming Dynasty was replaced by the Qing.

1420 CE - The Forbidden City is Completed

China has had many different capital cities over the years, and during the Ming Dynasty, it was decided that the imperial capital should be in Beijing. As no suitable accommodations for the emperor existed, construction began on a new palace. However, a simple palace was not deemed to be spacious enough to house much of the government and its officials. To deal with this problem, the palace was expanded to be an entire royal complex. The Forbidden City, as it eventually came to be known, was almost three-fifths of a mile long, and almost half a mile wide. The name Forbidden City was a reference to the fact that no person was allowed to enter, or leave, the city without the emperor's direct permission. As such, the vast bulk of the Chinese people would be barred from entry, as well as all but the highest ranking foreign emissaries. The Forbidden City was designed to elevate the emperor to an almost god-like status in the eyes of his people and visitors to China.

In modern times, the Forbidden City is the world's largest surviving collection of wooden buildings that remain in their original condition. The site has been deemed a World Heritage site due to its historical importance. As almost a million people were involved in its construction, the Forbidden Palace demonstrates how prosperous the Ming Dynasty was, in that it could use this many workers without causing adverse effects on the Chinese economy. Without doubt, the Forbidden Palace remains an important source of information about Chinese history.

1421 CE - Chinese Explorers First Reach North America

In 2002, a book was written that purported to turn world history on its head. *1421: The Year China Discovered the World*, written by Gavin Menzies, is a book in which Menzies makes the claim that Chinese sailors reached North America in 1421, which was 71 years before Columbus. Much of the evidence in the book is based on a map that is said to have been created in 1418 when Menzies claims the Chinese sailed east to the New World. Although much of Menzies book has been found to be false, conclusive written evidence that this event did not take place does not exist.

After the Qing Dynasty assumed rule in China, they set about destroying much of the record of Ming achievement. There is, however, a substantial record of the Ming fleet that explored the coast of Asia and Africa during the early 1400s, and so, while the Menzies theory may be false, Chinese exploration is not. Since the publication of the book in 2002, many people have come forward with claims of proof of Chinese exploration in North America. Although none have provided conclusive evidence, the theory has sparked a renewed interest in archaeology and history as people investigate the claims made by Menzies. Whether or not the Chinese reached North America in 1421 may never be conclusively proven, it is a testament to Ming ingenuity that such a possibility is even being debated.

1602 CE - The Dutch East India Company Starts Trading in China

In 1602, the Dutch created the first multinational corporation in history. Named the Dutch East India Company, the company was the first joint-stock company of its kind. The company, at its peak, employed tens of thousands of people to man the ships, ports, offices, and depots necessary to conduct international trade with China and other countries. To many westerners of the period, India and China were synonymous, which explains the name of the company. The company exported more than two million tons of goods from China between 1602 and 1796.

The success of the Dutch company inspired the British to create an eastern transportation corporation of their own, commonly referred to as the British East India Company. The English, however, took a slightly different approach to trade with the Chinese, and, desiring more tea than China was willing to provide, undertook means to force Chinese trade. As such, the British introduced opium to China, which would eventually lead to the Opium Wars in the late 1800s. In any event, the Dutch East India Company helped facilitate not only trade but also cultural diffusion. In fact, the Ming emperor became fascinated with European art, and slowly, these western artistic traditions began to find their way into Ming art, which is why much Ming porcelain contains European influence. Beyond this, the Dutch East India Company made China an international trading superpower, and much of Chinese culture was likewise transported west to Europe.

1644 CE - Qing Dynasty

In 1644, a group of Manchurians pushed south into China. As the forces traveled, many peasants began to revolt against the Ming, and eventually, the Manchurians established an empire in China, which they named the Qing Dynasty. Although complete unification in China did not occur until 1683, the Qing Dynasty was in full force by the end of 1644. The Qing was the last imperial dynasty in China, and they ruled until 1912. The Qing Dynasty was in power during the trade imbalance that led to the Opium Wars with Britain. The population of China doubled during the dynasty, and a major shift in population density occurred, as more and more people began moving out of rural areas into urban ones.

The Qing were also responsible for the Canton System, largely in response to the urbanization of China's population. The Qing made great advancements in poetry and calligraphy, as well as other art forms. At the same time, the Qing made strides in exporting quality porcelain, in order to keep up with increasing European demand. As more and more European crops were introduced in China, a movement sprang up to preserve Chinese cuisine and turn it into an art-form of its own. When the dynasty finally weakened, the populace moved toward a republic, bringing an end to one of the longest-running monarchies in history.

1757 CE - The Canton System Adopted

As international trade in China reached new heights, the emperors began to fear the influence of westerners on the culture and economy of China. As a result, in 1757, the Qing adopted a trade policy known as the Canton System. This system shifted all international trade in China to a single port, in the city of Canton (modern-day Guangzhou). This policy allowed Chinese officials to dictate prices of all goods being exported and imported, as the European merchants had no other trade options available to them.

As the British did not possess many goods of value to the Chinese, the British were most often forced to pay in silver for the products they desired to import to Britain and other European countries. In response, the British began exporting opium to China, knowing that the addictive qualities of the substance, coupled with a lack of Chinese-produced opium, would make the Chinese more likely to trade favorably. But with the Canton System in place, opium was only slowly spreading through China. When the balance of favor swung toward the Chinese due to the British desire for tea, the price for opium was increased, causing severe repercussions throughout China. This was the basis for the Opium Wars that would take place in the mid-to-late 1800s.

Modern History

"The Revolution is so that people can live, not so that they can die!"

—Lu Xun

1839 CE - First Opium War

As the dependency on opium began to rise in China, the Qing emperor was forced to take steps to curb the excesses of opium being seen throughout the empire. One of the emperor's trusted trade advisors confiscated more than two and a half million pounds of opium from the British without offering compensation for the loss. In turn, the British began shelling Chinese cities from their ships. The British, having a far superior navy eventually caused heavy enough casualties that the Chinese signed the Treaty of Nanking in 1842. The treaty forced China to open up multiple cities for trade, to pay for the cost of the war, and to turn control of Hong Kong over to the British. Rather than having any more destruction occur, the Qing Emperor Daoguang signed the treaty.

This treaty marked the beginning of a period in Chinese history known as the "Century of Humiliation" in which the once-proud Chinese civilization began to decline and was no longer viewed as a world power by other nations. The Treaty of Nanking was fairly broad and general and did not provide guidance in terms of enforcement. As such, tensions rose between both sides, and a Second Opium War was fought between 1856 and 1860. When the second war ended, the Tianjin was signed, explicitly covering the details of reparations and trade that had been attempted with the Treaty of Nanking.

1900 CE - Boxer Rebellion

After the Treaty of Nanking and Tianjin, discontent among the Chinese people began to emerge. In 1900, a militia known as the Boxers emerged and attempted to invade Beijing to force the government to go to war with the European nations that held China in trade slavery at the time. The Boxers held foreigners in Beijing under siege, and when the European armies were initially defeated, those same nations sent 20,000 troops to China. Eventually, the European armies defeated the Boxers.

China was forced to pay reparations to the other nations involved, and the cost of yearly reparations was greater than the government collected in taxes in a year. To further weaken the Chinese, the Boxer Protocol (treaty) allowed for the stationing of foreign troops in China, in order to prevent further rebellions. The actions of the Chinese government in not fully supporting the Boxers caused many civilians to become angry with their government and begin thinking about the replacement of the monarchical form of government.

1911 CE - The Republic of China Holds First Elections

In 1911, an uprising against the Qing Dynasty took place. Known as the Wuchang Uprising, this rebellion put an end to the Chinese Empire in 1912. As the uprising gained momentum, the group founded the Republic of China. In order to establish credibility as a republic, presidential elections were held in 1911. Sun Yat-sen was elected the first president of the Republic of China. But, by 1912, he was replaced after losing a parliamentary election. In 1916, the military took control of the government. The army was led by Yuan Shikai, and upon his death, the republic fractured into several small factions, each controlled by a warlord. In 1925, a group of Chinese nationalists formed the Kuomintang (KMT) party in an attempt to bring legitimate government back to China. The KMT was led by General Chiang Kai-shek. The KMT found itself at odds with the Communist Party of China, until 1934, at which time the KMT pushed the communist forces north, a move known as the Long March. Despite the troubles faced by the Republic of China during its short tenure, the Republic is noted for having transitioned China away from monarchy towards republic and democracy.

1934 CE - The Long March

During the conflict between the KMT and Communist Party during the early 1930s, it became clear that the

KMT forces outmanned those of the communists (or Reds). As such, in 1934, the various Red Armies began a strategic march north and west in the hopes of escaping the KMT. During the march, which was as long as approximately 9,000 kilometers, Mao Zedong began his rise to power. His leadership under the tremendously difficult conditions gave the army a great appreciation for him and gave Mao a deeper understanding of the skills necessary to lead a vast nation of people. After the Long March was completed, the KMT took control of the government. This success would be short-lived, however, as the Japanese invaded China in 1937.

In order to repel the Japanese forces, which would not be fully accomplished until the Sino-Japanese War's end, the KMT was forced to ally itself with the Red Army, which put the Red Army in a position of great strength after the war. When that happened, Mao was in a place of authority from which he could help the Red Army (and Communist Party) seize control of China.

1937 CE - Nanking Massacre

In 1937, seeking mineral resources, the Japanese invaded China. In December, the Japanese conquered the Chinese capital city of Nanking (variously Nanjing). Over the first six weeks of the occupation, the Japanese murdered anywhere from 40,000-300,000 Chinese citizens. Beyond that, an estimated 20,000 women were raped, and the number of children and elderly women who were raped has not been accurately counted. The actions of the occupying soldiers were so reprehensible that the event has also been called the "Rape of Nanking." The reason for the wildly disparate casualty estimates is that the Japanese destroyed most of the records containing information about this time period, leaving little firsthand information for historians to uncover. There is even a story that was told at the time (and which a judge in 2005 said could not legally be proven false) that a pair of Japanese soldiers held a contest between themselves to see who could kill 100 civilians first, using nothing but a sword.

After the Japanese surrender in late 1945, the Chinese held tribunals to determine the guilt of officers involved in the Nanking Massacre. Only seven soldiers who were tried for the massacre were found guilty of a capital crime, and those seven were executed. Others were found guilty of lesser sentences, but not put to death. Several memorials have been built to commemorate the suffering of the Chinese people during the Nanking Massacre.

1949 CE - The Republic of China Moves to Taiwan

After the Japanese surrender at the end of World War II, China had to begin the monumental task of rebuilding and repairing the damage done during the occupation. Because the Red Army had allied itself with the KMT during the war, the Reds had gained a great deal of popularity. With war's end, the civil war between the KMT and the Reds resumed in 1946. This time, the Reds were successful, and in 1949, the KMT government was forced to flee.

Mao Zedong and the communists established the People's Republic of China on the mainland. The KMT forces left mainland China and settled on the island of Taiwan. Once there, the KMT re-established the Republic of China. From that moment on, the Republic of China (ROC) claimed independence from China and sought to gain international recognition of its independence. On the other side, the People's Republic of China (PRC) claimed that Taiwan and the ROC were simply a rebellious faction of the PRC and that the ROC ought not to have standing among the independent nations of the world.

As this fracture occurred during the Cold War, the United States and other world powers were hesitant to acknowledge the independence of the ROC for fear of angering the PRC, and potentially, its communist ally, Russia. As such, major western powers began to trade with the ROC, without giving formal acknowledgment of its status. Although this move angered the PRC, it was unwilling to go to war with the west over this unspoken recognition. Even today, this issue remains unsettled by China and Taiwan, and although hostility breaks out occasionally, neither side seems willing to commit the resources necessary to permanently settle the issue.

1958 CE - The Great Leap Forward

Throughout the 1950s China continued to lag behind the rest of the world powers as it struggled to rebuild itself and its industry. Mao Zedong proposed a massive agricultural and industrial recovery program to modernize China. Named Great Leap Forward, the plan was supposed to mimic Russia, Germany, or the United States during their various times of rebuilding. However, Mao planned to privatize heavy industry like steelmaking, so that large quantities of materials could be produced with vast expenditures of capital on the part of the government. And so, heavy industry was turned over to the cottage-industry of centuries past. The notion was flawed from the beginning. Steelmaking is not an endeavor well-suited to home-furnace use. As such, the steel produced was virtually worthless, setting back industry by several years. In addition, the Great Leap Forward collectivized farms, meaning that farming was done by groups, not individuals. Sadly, this method of farming is not well-suited to a big, industrial society. Unsurprisingly then, the Great Leap Forward was an economic and social disaster.

A famine struck during the Great Leap, and so, without technology to aid the people, an estimated 18-45 million people died during the years 1958-1962. Put into perspective, 60 million people died during World War II, and that counts non-combat deaths associated with the war (sickness, construction accidents, etc.). In other words, the Great Leap Forward killed three-fourths as many people as World War II, and in only one country. The Great Leap was so catastrophic that Communist Party in China turned its back on Mao and began plans to oust him from government, which, in turn, led to the Cultural Revolution.

1966 CE - The Cultural Revolution

Mao Zedong, after the failure of the Great Leap Forward, was viewed as a pariah and the rest of the communist government sought to oust him from power. In 1966, Mao instituted the Cultural Revolution. The stated purpose of the revolution was to purge any remaining capitalist or traditionalist thought from the citizenry, and in its place, establish the Cult of Mao, as the center of Chinese thought, and life. Mao established his "cult of personality"—that is, Mao himself became the central idea of life in China. Mao had millions of copies of his "Little Red Book" distributed, and persons found without it on their person were subject to punishment. Further, Mao appealed to the youth in China, and very quickly the Red Guards were created from a corps of teens.

During the revolution, citizens were encouraged to report any "non-Maoist" thought or activity to the Red Guard, who would take appropriate action against the violator. Those who reported violations were often given rewards and positions of authority. This means that from 1966-1976 (at the end of the revolution) much of the productive activity in China came to a halt as people were too afraid to do anything creative or thoughtful. An estimated 30 million people died during the revolution, meaning that as many as 75 million people died due to decisions directly made by Mao Zedong. This startling number means that Mao was responsible for almost as many deaths as Hitler and Stalin combined, making Mao one of the most violent leaders in world history. The Cultural Revolution came to an end in 1976, when Mao died after a series of heart-attacks.

1972 CE - Nixon Visits China

Upon assuming the presidency in the United States, Richard Nixon sought to formalize a relationship with the People's Republic of China, something that had not been done up to that point. In 1972, Nixon traveled to China. From February 21-28, Nixon and his wife toured the country and had serious discussions with various Chinese diplomats. During this time, the American press corps that had traveled with Nixon reported back the first image of China in approximately 20 years. Nixon met with Mao, and thanks to the productivity of that meeting as well as the other diplomatic meetings, relations between the two countries were normalized.

Due in large part to Nixon's trip, China shifted Cold War alliances away from Russia to the United States. This shift in balance would play a role in the eventual fall of the Soviet Union. More immediately, Nixon's visit to China paved the way for trade relations which would be of great benefit to both countries. Of final note, Nixon's visit allowed the U.S. and China to peacefully disagree over the issue of Taiwan, without fear of either side getting involved in a military action relating to Taiwan.

1989 CE - Tiananmen Square Protests

In April 1989, a group of students gathered in Tiananmen Square (located outside the Forbidden City) to mourn the death of Hu Yaobang, the former party secretary. Yaobang had been liberal and sought to reform China's government. As many as one million students gathered to mourn Yaobang and demand changes from the government, including free speech and free press. As the protest spread to 400 cities, Deng Xiaoping, the leader of China after Mao's death, opted to use force to put down the Tiananmen Square protest. As many as 250,000 troops were sent to the Square to maintain order.

On June 4, 1989, the army moved to clear the square of protesters. During the protest and clearing of the square, somewhere between 300 and 1,000 people were killed. There is no single official count of casualties, and every source gives a different total. Most agree to the range of 300 to 1,000 dead. This massacre, as it came to be known, posed an international setback to China. The protest had had widespread coverage, and so the whole world was made aware of the actions that had taken place. Tourism declined in the wake of the events, and the World Bank held up several loans to the Chinese. The protests demonstrated to the world the level of difficulty China was having maintaining itself as a communist country despite the growing internal pressure to move towards democratic government.

2002 CE - SARS Outbreak

In November 2002, an outbreak of what was believed to be Severe Acute Respiratory Syndrome occurred near Hong Kong. SARS is a virus that attacks the respiratory system and has approximately a 10% mortality rate in infected patients. The relatively high mortality rate, coupled with the ease and mode of transmission (SARS is both fluid-borne and airborne), made SARS a potential threat to a large population across the world. By early 2003, people from 37 countries had been infected with SARS, and fears of a global pandemic were manifest. By July 2003, the World Health Organization claimed that the disease had been contained, and although four cases were discovered in 2004, no cases have been reported since that time.

SARS demonstrated for the first time the very real possibility that, thanks to rapid global transit, viruses that might otherwise have a small impact could potentially become threatening to humans across the world. This almost-pandemic taught the world health community about its own weaknesses and gave countries the opportunity to plan and prepare for a true pandemic disease. These procedures were put in place during the Ebola outbreak in 2015.

2003 CE - First Manned Chinese Spaceflight

On October 15, 2003, China launched its first manned spacecraft into outer space. Named the Shenzhou 5, the craft was piloted by Yang Liwei. The Shenzhou 5 followed four unmanned Shenzhou launches, which were designed to test the craft's spaceworthiness. Liwei completed 14 orbits of the earth during just over 21 hours in space. This flight was significant because it marked only the third country in history to send astronauts into space on a vehicle created in the same country. During the flight, Liwei verified command and control systems, as well as environmental and housekeeping systems. This flight paved the way for Shenzhou 6, which carried two astronauts into orbit for five days.

The progress of the Chinese space program demonstrates that China has once again become a world power in technology and trade and that its space program is among those at the forefront of space exploration. Currently, NASA and the China National Space Administration (CNSA) are partners working together on the International Space Station Program along with many other countries. This program, along with others, is a testament to a shift in Chinese policy that once favored secrecy and exclusion, but now favors transparency and openness towards other nations in the world.

2008 CE - Beijing Olympics Held

In August 2008, Beijing hosted the 29th Summer Olympics. Over 200 National Olympic Committees sent almost 11,000 athletes to compete in the 302 events of the Summer Games. A record 86 countries won at least one medal during the games, with the United States leading the final medal count with 110 to China's 100 medals. China won the most gold medals with a total of 51. During the games, many news outlets made much ado over the poor air quality in Beijing, with athletes often needing to wear personal breathing masks when not in competition. China has struggled with environmental issues as it has been rapidly industrialized since the 1970s.

Despite that, the games were considered a success, with Michael Phelps, an American swimmer, winning eight gold medals—the most ever won by a single athlete in a single Olympics. In order to improve times, Speedo and other manufacturers enlisted NASA's help with wind tunnel simulations to produce the LZR Racer swimsuit. This suit was so advanced that of sixty-seven total Olympic records in swimming, only two remained unbroken after the Olympics was complete. It was even banned from the 2012 London Olympic Games.

Overall, the Beijing Games were completed successfully, and they demonstrated to the world that as it had been for so many centuries in the past, China was once again a world leader, and deserving of the respect that it had earned over its long, varied history.

Made in the USA
San Bernardino, CA
25 March 2019